Creative and Thoughtful GIFT GIVING

text **Leah Ingram**

photography **Aimée Herring**

styling **Lauren Hunter**

GIFT BOOKS
from Hallmark

BOK5516

HALLMARK

Art Director **Kevin Swanson**
Editor **Jeff Morgan**

WELDON OWEN

Chief Executive Officer **John Owen**
President & Chief Operating Officer **Terry Newell**
Chief Financial Officer **Christine E. Munson**
Vice President, Publisher **Roger Shaw**
Vice President, Creative Director **Gaye Allen**
Vice President, International Sales **Stuart Laurence**

Senior Art Director **Emma Boys**
Designer **Renée Myers**
Illustrations **Salli Swindell**

Managing Editor **Elizabeth Dougherty**
Project Editor **Kendra Smith**
Contributing Editor **Maria Behan**
Editorial Assistant **Lucie Parker**

Production Director **Chris Hemesath**
Color Manager **Teri Bell**
Photo Coordinator **Meghan Hildebrand**

Published by Gift Books from Hallmark, a division of
Hallmark Cards, Inc., Kansas City, MO 64141.
Visit us at www.hallmark.com.

Produced by Weldon Owen Inc., 814 Montgomery Street,
San Francisco, CA 94133.
Visit us at www.weldonowen.com.

BOK5516

Separated in Canada by Embassy Graphics
Printed and bound in China by Leo Paper
First printed 2007
10 9 8 7 6 5 4 3 2 1
ISBN 978-1-59530-147-5

contents

gifts with heart—and style

Good things come in all sorts of packages. And when those packages contain gifts, they're all the more delightful when presented in creative and thoughtful ways—ways that show recipients just how much you care about them. We've filled *Creative and Thoughtful Gift Giving* with easy-to-do ideas for wrapping presents in memorable ways. Choose the ones that inspire you, and mix and match them to suit any occasion or individual. Whether it's Mother's Day or Christmas, whether you're giving a present for a birthday or flowers to say "thanks," have fun adding your own special touches. Sometimes it really is more enjoyable to give than to receive!

ideas for her

Many women have an eye for detail, and pretty much all of them treasure thoughtfulness. So when you give a gift to a special woman in your life, present it with a personalized flourish to show her just how well you know her and how much you care. Package a gift especially for your mom, sister, daughter, or friend—and watch her face light up.

add some sparkle

Whether vintage or vintage-inspired, a sparkling brooch adds glamour and polish to a gift and becomes an instant keepsake. And because brooches have built-in pins, it's easy as can be to attach these beautiful baubles to a ribbon.

costume collection
For a selection of brooches (above), raid an old jewelry box, purchase new pins made in a vintage style, or scoop up some treasures at garage sales or online. Look for colors and patterns that you like, and don't worry too much if there's a stone missing here or there.

pretty palette
Use the gems in a multihued brooch (left) to define a color combination for wrapping a gift. Blue grosgrain ribbon, striped wired ribbon, and a block-print tag work together by playing off the pin's colors. The gray-blue raw silk covering the box peeks through underneath.

understated elegance
Keep the wrapping simple to focus attention on a starburst brooch (right). The directions of the ribbons echo the brooch's star shape: wide moss green satin bands crisscross one way, narrow metallic silver ones another.

pretty in pink

Create an eye-catching present by decorating it in the same happy family of rosy hues. Different shades, textures, and patterns of pink—finished with details like ribbons, buttons, and blooms—make a statement that's both bold and sweet.

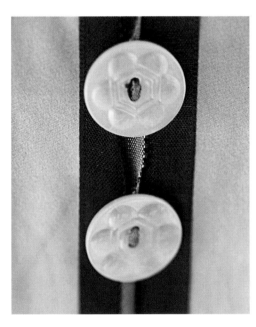

buttoned-up box

Start with a square box wrapped in marbled or other textured paper (see page 134 for tips).

1 Wrap a strand of the widest ribbon around the box. Trim to size and affix to the bottom with double-sided tape. Put a strand of thinner ribbon on top of the first ribbon, trim, and affix.

2 Wrap the thinnest ribbon around the box to measure and trim to size. Using a needle with a large eye, thread several buttons evenly on each side, then wrap the thin ribbon over the other two. Affix to the bottom with double-sided tape.

3 Stack strands of all three ribbons, from widest to thinnest, and wrap once around the box in the other direction, covering the taped ribbon ends on the bottom and leaving the ends long at the top. Thread buttons onto the thinnest ribbon.

4 Tie the three strands of ribbons in a single bow, keeping them stacked, and trim the ends evenly.

5 Trim the flower's stem short and tuck it under the bow. If it will be a while until you give the gift, place the flower in a florist's vial filled with water and hide the vial under the ribbons.

a gem of a gift

A small box often suggests a big surprise inside, especially when you give jewelry. Make a petite package all the more special by adding an extra touch like fabric lining on the inside or a tiny bouquet of paper flowers on the outside.

beaded embellishments
Cut-glass beads attached to a box hint at its contents (above). Metallic gift wrap and a beaded tag echo the jewel theme. Also consider decorating packages with pearl, silver, rhinestone, or other beads.

jewelry box lining
Adding a simple paper and fabric lining (left) instantly upgrades a boxed gift of jewelry. Crisscross pieces of tissue paper at the bottom of the box. (Snip with pinking shears for nicely finished edges.) Use tulle or other netting to cushion and secure the jewelry inside the box.

ring-size bouquet
Scale a presentation bouquet to the size of a ring box by wrapping a bunch of small paper flowers with tulle and securing with ribbon (right). A pretty piece of candy or a fresh flower also makes a nice gift attachment.

corset a box

Lacing paper like a corset around a box is an easy way to add feminine style to a present. It's especially appropriate when the package you've laced up to resemble a vintage piece of lingerie contains a silky little something inside.

lovely laces

Lace up a box to resemble a corset (left) and hark back to days gone by. Wrap a piece of paper around the box, making sure the ends don't meet. Hole-punch or grommet the ends, then thread with ribbon like a shoelace and tie a bow. Add a whimsical paper cutout of a bra.

sweet sachet

A sachet for a dresser drawer (right) is a sweet-smelling addition to a gift of clothing—whether it's a wool sweater or pink panties. Use a ready-made sachet, or put potpourri in a lace square, bring up the sides, and tie with ribbon.

treat her right

Show how much you care about her—and her well-being—by putting together a collection of items she can use to pamper herself. Fill an enamel basin to the brim with spa indulgences, such as bath salts, body brushes, and post-pedicure flip-flops.

thoughtful themes

When you package themed gifts together, use your knowledge of the recipient's preferences to come up with the perfect personal collection. For instance, create a spa kit for a friend who loves lavender, complete with products in her favorite scent and color.

● Opt for an enamel soaking bowl as an alternative to a basket and fill it with spa supplies, such as a soft towel, a pair of flip-flops, and body brushes.

● Package bath products separately. Remove any tags or plastic wrap, then place each item in its own clear bag for protection and easy identification. Tie on a straightforward label like "scrub."

● You can also base a themed gift on a favorite hobby: pack a canvas shopping bag with spices and kitchen gadgets for a cook, or fill a bird feeder with seeds and field guides for a bird lover.

wrapped up in romance

Giving a gift to your sweetheart is a wonderful excuse to be sentimental. Offer a key to your heart (literally), quote a sonnet, or say "I love you" in another language. Then personalize it with your own private terms of endearment.

say "I love you"

Tell a special someone how you feel in a new way.

Chinese •	*Wo ai ni*
Danish •	*Jeg elsker dig*
French •	*Je t'aime*
German •	*Ich liebe dich*
Greek •	*S'agapo*
Italian •	*Ti amo*
Spanish •	*Te quiero*

key to your heart
When you're packaging a present for your sweetie, go ahead and wear your heart on your sleeve with lots of Xs and Os (left). Fasten a glass drawer knob to the lid of a fabric-covered box, and hang a symbolic key from it.

poem on paper
Say more with flowers by wrapping a bouquet with a meaningful message (right). Print out a romantic poem, handwrite a personal sentiment, or choose gift wrap with an appropriate saying. Envelop with a layer of sheer fabric so the words peek through.

speak the language of flowers

Historically, blooms have conveyed specific sentiments. Revisit this tradition when you give flowers or a flower-inspired gift by including a card that explains the meaning.

flower and meaning	card message	gift idea
Carnation Admiration, maternal love	*Carnations mean admiration. And I want you to know just how much I admire you.*	Arrange bunches of carnations in a pair of brightly colored children's rain boots.
Chrysanthemum Cheerfulness	*Chrysanthemums bring cheer. Hope this brightens your day!*	Present a container of chrysanthemum tea with a small ceramic teapot.
Daffodil Regard, respect	*Daffodils stand for high regard. Please know how highly I think of you.*	Place daffodil bulbs in a fabric bag that's the same color as the flowers will be.
Dahlia Gratitude	*People send dahlias to express their gratitude. Thank you so much!*	Decorate a wrapped gift box with blooms, ribbon, and paper leaves (left).
Gardenia Joy	*Gardenias mean joy. You bring so much joy to others; here's some for you, too.*	Set a gardenia-scented candle in a basket filled with gardenia blossoms.
Iris Compliments, symbol of France	*A symbol of France, an iris also says "my compliments." Here's to you, mon amie!*	Put a stalk of iris in a Champagne flute and pair it with a bottle of French Champagne.
Pansy Loving thoughts	*These pansies stand for the loving thoughts that I'm sending your way.*	Give a set of note cards or a journal with pansies pressed in the paper.
Rose Love, friendship (pink roses)	*Pink roses honor friendship. Here's a gift to show how much I cherish ours.*	Fill a pink gift bag with a rose-petal sachet, a bottle of rose water, and rose-scented soap.
Sunflower Pride, admiration	*People give sunflowers when they're proud. You know what? I am . . . of you!*	To mark an accomplishment or a kind deed, give your child a bag of sunflower seeds.
Sweet pea Farewell, departure	*Sweet peas signify farewell. I'm really going to miss you. Best of luck!*	For friends who are going away, put a bouquet in a tote bag that they can take along.
Zinnia Thoughts of friends	*Zinnias convey thoughts of friends. Just thinking of you, my wonderful friend.*	Present the flowers in a clear vase. Use food coloring to tint the water to match their hue.

blooms in a box

Next time you bring someone flowers, tuck a water-filled container into a colorfully wrapped box as an alternative to a vase. Your blooms will stay fresh until you give them—and once you do, they're all ready to display and enjoy.

flower power

Flowers often make the ideal gift, since they say everything from "I love you" to "I'm sorry." (See page 25 for more on the meaning of flowers.) Consider giving a bouquet that's already arranged and watered in a decorative box.

• Here, fuchsia and celadon hydrangeas reside cheerfully with geranium leaves in a fabric-covered box originally designed for CD storage. Florist's foam, soaked in water and set in a plastic bag, secures and refreshes the arrangement.

• A gift tag that reads "Thanks a bunch" slides into the slot for labeling the box. Grosgrain ribbon with stripes in the flowers' hues ties it all together.

• When mixing flowers, choose colors and blooms that work well in a garden, like red tulips and orange gerbera daisies or purple petunias and yellow marigolds.

• You can present a bouquet, a potted plant, or other greenery in a gift box, a hatbox, or just about any box that's the right size. Cover with pretty paper or fabric to complete the look.

make mother's day magic

A Mother's Day gift from a child is already special, but it becomes even more adorable—and very personal—when you add photographs or artwork. Mom or Grandma will find herself treasuring the gift even before she opens it.

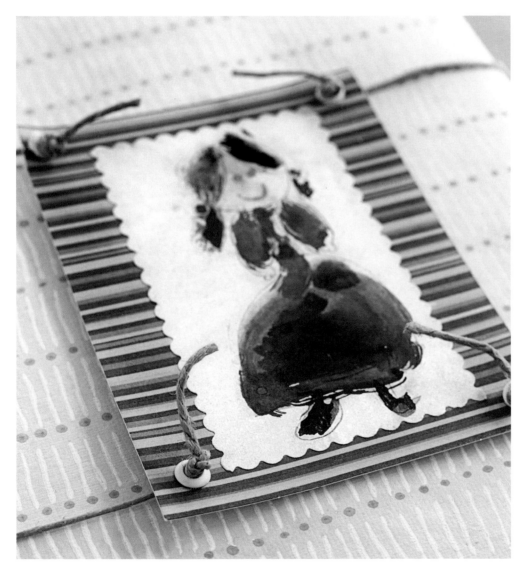

involve the kids

Make decorating gift wrap for Mom a family event by having the kids join in.

- Let them use rubber stamps or stamps you cut from apples or potatoes.

- Give them free rein to color plain wrapping paper with crayons.

- Have them select and attach stickers that reflect one of Mom's interests.

mini masterpiece

A child's painting or drawing can be both a decoration (left) and a gift in its own right. Frame artwork by gluing it to a larger piece of patterned or colored paper. Punch elastic cording through the corners and secure around the box.

from all of us

Photos combined with name tags (far left) make it easy to picture who's giving a gift, which can be an especially nice touch for a special someone who lives far away. Copy photos together, cut the paper into a strip, and attach it to the package, or simply tape on snapshots.

ideas for him

Men like gifts—and gift presentations—that show how much

you "get" them. So let his personality and style guide you as you put

together packages that are whimsical, striking, or practical. Whether it's

his birthday, Father's Day, or a romantic occasion, the man in your life

will appreciate the personal touch as much as the present.

hardware-store finds

Your local hardware store is a treasure trove of package embellishments that do double duty as gifts. Nuts, clamps, and other hardware gadgets can be terrific tools when it comes time to wrap your favorite handyman's present.

bubble it up

For a present that pops, wrap a set of tools or other odd-shaped items in bubble wrap (above). Keep the hardware theme going by using springs and copper wire as "ribbons."

clamp it down

Package your gift in polka-dot paper and use a C-clamp (left) as a "bow." Look around the hardware store for other items, such as tiny A-clamps and painter's or duct tape, that you can use creatively when wrapping gifts.

mesh it together

Wrap a bouquet of screwdrivers in window screening (far left) and cinch it with a hose clamp. A metal chain secures the gift tag, which is actually a paper key tag with metal trim. You can group other tools, such as flashlights or wrenches, in a similar way.

playing with patterns

Mix and match striped paper, ribbons, and tags to create a one-of-a-kind package. Feel free to experiment: tie a knot instead of a bow, play around with shades in a cool palette, or get bold with bright, preppy colors.

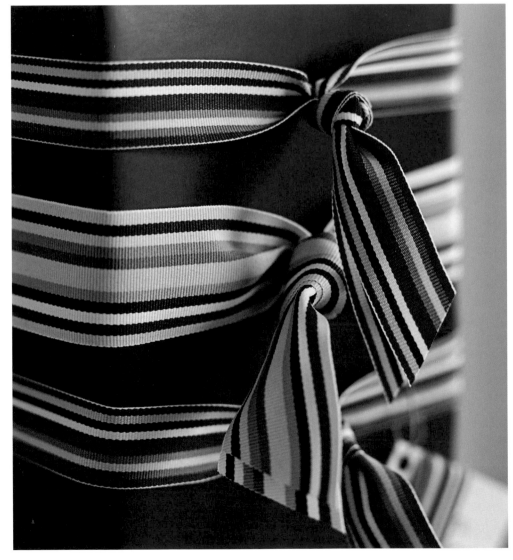

tagged to match

Showcase crisp colors by using the same patterned ribbon to adorn both a package and a plain white tag (above). Creating a coordinating gift tag is a great way to use ribbon scraps and to make a package look finished.

knots aplenty

For a simple but fresh ribbon treatment, knot three strands across a package (left). Here, the center one is a wider variation. Preppy-striped grosgrain ribbons are a spot-on complement to the cobalt blue paper because of the blue bands running through them.

mix it up

Wrap a pair of packages in striped papers and ribbon (right). The secret to this successful mix: all the elements have stripes and contain cool colors, like light neutrals, black, and baby blue. You can also combine other patterns, such as checks or plaids, that have similar colors.

A FEW OF YOUR FAVORITE THINGS

tailor-made packages

Clothing can inspire ideas for gift decoration or can even be the wrapping for a present. Echo the rivets of jeans with copper paper clips, or use a striped shirt as a stand-in for paper.

fashion-forward colors

When giving clothes, coordinate the color of the wrap with the gift inside the box. The wrap can match the main colors of the outfit or pick up on a detail. Strands of copper spiral paper clips (left), for example, reflect the metallic rivets on a great pair of jeans.

all dressed up

Clothe a gift box with a striped dress shirt (right). A fabric ribbon literally ties this outfit together. A belt or tie would also work as "ribbon." Other wrap options include fabric or fabric-inspired paper (see pages 120–121).

a little romance

Who says men are afraid of romance? If you wrap a romantic gift in a way that's sentimental, affectionate, or fondly teasing, he's bound to melt. Just match the package to the gift and the personality of the recipient. Go on, flirt a little!

personalize a box

Think of a brown kraft box as a blank canvas.

• Decorate with doodles and hand-drawn pictures, like your initials in a heart (as if the box were a tree).

• Glue on candy hearts with romantic sayings.

• Bend pipe cleaners into heart shapes and attach them with yarn.

memory lane
Create one-of-a-kind wrapping paper by copying snapshots of a trip you've taken together (left). Decorate with a souvenir, such as a sand dollar tied on with red raffia. You can also print digital photos in black and white or sepia.

message of love
This simple brown kraft box tied with red-striped ribbon (right) makes a statement. A cutout heart, drawer pull, and rubber-stamped letters all add up to say "Hey, good lookin'—open me."

especially for dad

Remind him that he's the best father ever by turning to your kids for inspiration in wrapping his gift. Showcase a child's masterpiece or capture a little one's tiny footprints.

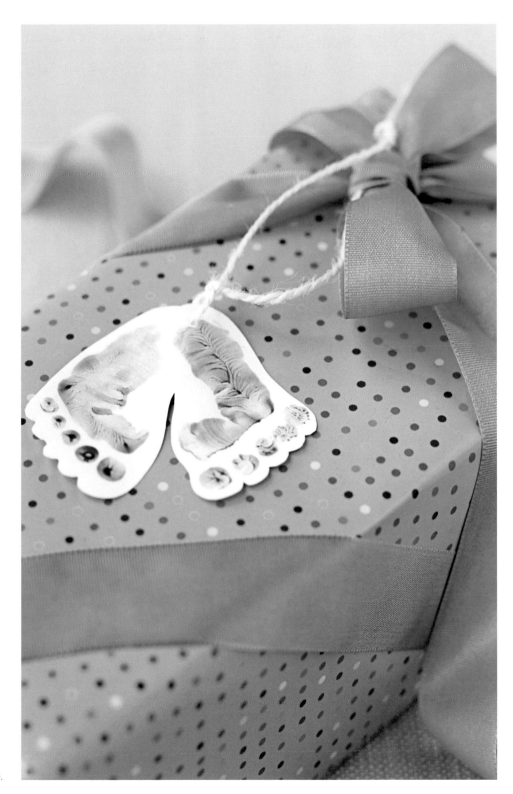

keepsake box

An original family portrait (left), courtesy of a son or daughter, adorns a gift for Dad. White kraft paper covering a shoe box lid provides a canvas for your young artistic genius, transforming a box into a keepsake. (Wrap the box bottom separately.) Have the kids pick out a cheery ribbon they like.

feet first

A child's footprints stamped on paper and paired as a gift tag (right) will send Dad head over heels. It also will serve as a memento to remind him just how small those feet used to be. You can also stamp a child's footprints or handprints on gift wrap.

birthdays

Presenting a creatively wrapped gift makes a birthday girl

or boy feel the way we all should on our big day: like a star. Whether

the recipient is a child or a child at heart, taking a clever approach to

wrapping a gift—for instance, by attaching unexpected accessories—will

ensure that your present is the one he or she wants to open first.

special attachments

When you adorn a birthday gift package with fun additions, such as glow-in-the-dark stars, a ribbon butterfly, or colorful shoelaces in place of ribbons, you add visual interest to the package—and an extra gift for the lucky birthday boy or girl.

butterfly kiss
A ribbon butterfly (above) alights on a polka-dot package. To form the wings, circle wired ribbon into four separate loops, pinch the middle of the loops, and secure with a pipe cleaner. Twist the pipe cleaner to look like the body and antennae. Attach the butterfly to the gift with another piece of pipe cleaner.

star bright
For a celestial theme, decorate blue paper with glow-in-the-dark stars (left). Attach with double-sided tape so their adhesive backing can be used later. Circle a round gift tag with pipe cleaners to look like the rings of a planet.

lace it up
Tie brightly patterned shoelaces over solid-colored wrapping paper (right). You can also embellish packages with other accessories, such as hair ribbons or candy necklaces, for a similar effect.

think outside the box

With kids, sometimes the box a gift comes in provides part of the fun. What child hasn't turned a cardboard box into a castle or a fort? Take that concept a step further by transforming a gift box into a roller skate, a sailboat, or another playful object.

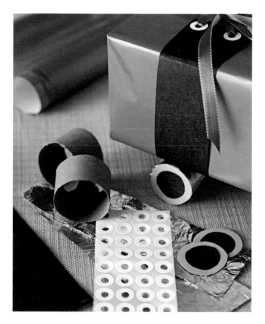

Pick bright and colorful materials for this box.

- Rectangular box
- Wrapping paper
- Construction paper
- Hole punch
- Paper reinforcements
- Double-sided tape
- Ribbon or shoelaces
- Cardboard tube
- Glue
- Aluminum foil

roller skate box

To craft a roller skate, start with a rectangular box and wrap it in solid-colored paper.

1 To make bands to hold the "laces," cut wide strips of construction paper, hole-punch them, and place paper reinforcements over the holes.

2 Wrap the paper bands around the box, securing them with double-sided tape as you go. Thread ribbons or shoelaces through the holes, as you would lace up a roller skate, and tie them in a bow.

3 For wheels, cut pieces from a cardboard tube, cover with foil, and glue on circles of construction paper. Attach to the box with double-sided tape.

sailboat variation

Poke a hole in the top of the box. Tape a piece of polystyrene or cork under the hole on the inside of the box. Wrap the box. Push a bamboo skewer "mast" with paper-triangle sails through the hole. Add paper waves. Finish with fish and an anchor.

clever containers

Expect squeals of delight at a kid's birthday party when you give a present in an unexpected container. Allow your inner child free rein as you transform a party hat into a gift bag or morph a pillow box into a friendly monster.

hats off

Party hats (left and above), whether felt or paper, can double as festive containers for small presents. Maintain an element of surprise by wrapping a gift in tissue paper and tying it with a colorful ribbon before placing it in the hat. Also consider using containers such as lunch boxes, tote bags, sand pails, or baskets.

monster mash

Transform a pillow box into a monster (far left) that holds a surprise—perhaps a gift card—inside. Glue on spiky paper fins and attach a pink paper tongue. Add some googly eyes for a giggle, and make them stand out by attaching them to cutout circles. You can also craft other creatures, like a frog, a lion, or a cow.

fun-filled goody bags

Assemble a collection of great party favors—and win the prize for "most fun mom"—by putting take-home gifts in nifty containers that play on the party's theme.

girl power

Give girly-girl goody bags (right) that will send the boys running. Fill plastic bowls with treats from the cosmetic aisle, like nail polish, ponytail holders, bath beads, and lip gloss. Hole-punch the sides, add a headband handle, and secure with twine. (These bowls came pleated, but any lightweight plastic bowl in the right size will work.)

drink it up

A plastic beverage cup (far right) is just the right size for goodies such as toy animals, a bouncy ball, and, of course, a crazy straw. Plus, the whole package fits into a cup holder during the ride home from the party.

presto! wrap it fast

Busy lives often call for swift birthday gift wrapping. Even if you have to run from a soccer game to a surprise party, you can assemble packages quickly if you use decorations such as yarn or stickers in place of tape to fasten gift wrap.

quick-wrap tricks

To wrap a gift lickety-split, keep it simple.

• Choose double-sided gift wrap. Wrap the gift with one side. Turn over a strip and loop a band around.

• Make it all about the bow. Use a plain box with an extra-special ribbon.

• Midnight and out of paper? Use calendar or magazine pages—even foil.

tissue comets
Gather several layers of tissue paper around a small present and tie together with chunky yarn (left). If you're giving a gift that has many parts, wrap each one separately to extend the excitement of unwrapping. This easy technique also applies to gifts that are odd shapes (see page 137 for more tips).

stick to it
Rows of square and round stickers (right) do two jobs in one, decorating solid-colored gift wrap and holding it in place. Select stickers in various colors, shapes, and sizes. Make creative patterns, or just stick them on in a row.

gussy up gift bags

A gift bag is a quick and easy way to give just about any present. To make the presentation extra special, replace the handles with ribbons or use shredded paper "grass" as filler. To decorate a gift bag so it seems custom-made for the recipient, attach a photo strip that brings back happy memories.

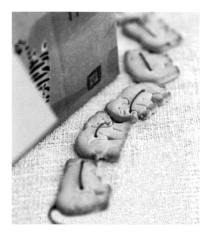

that's entertainment!

Plugged-in people love getting movies and music. Think outside the jewel case by wrapping your gift to offer clues about what's inside—for example, decorating a set of DVDs or videos about animals with playful lions, tigers, and bears.

animals on parade

Wrap a set of animal-themed DVDs or videos in zoo-inspired paper (left). Herd animal crackers with embroidery floss (above), stringing it through existing holes or ones you make with a needle. Using gift wrap with animal patterns, such as tiger or zebra stripes, is another way to run with the animal theme.

it's a wrap

Decorate a gift bag with a film library loan tag (right) and personalize it with the recipient's name. (You can buy a preprinted personal library kit online or print your own lending cards.) Keep the contents in the bag by replacing the handles with chopsticks. Use the same approach for wrapping CDs or books.

judge a book by its cover

Book lovers treasure additions to their personal libraries. Let them read between the lines by using packaging that reflects the topic of the book inside—a newspaper's food section for a cookbook, for example, or a map for a travel guidebook.

going places
Get someone ready to hit the road by using a map to wrap a guidebook (above). Photocopy a map or use a retired one, like this topographic one from the U.S. Geological Survey. You can add a mini compass to point this gift even further in the right direction.

help a garden grow
Floral paper is ideal wrap for a gardening book (left). Plant an idea of the gift that's inside by attaching packets of seeds to a burlap bow as a decoration and an extra gift for the green-thumbed recipient.

bon appétit
A cookbook wrapped in the pages of a newspaper's food section (right) is sure to whet someone's appetite for what's inside. Cook up even more excitement by tying on tubes of spices with ribbons. Or attach a related kitchen gadget, like a garlic press on a pasta cookbook.

birthstone inspirations

Personalize a birthday gift by relating it to the recipient's birthstone.
But rather than giving jewelry, give a gift inspired by the gem.

birthstone	gift idea	birthstone	gift idea
January Garnet	Give anything that suggests the fiery hue of this stone: deep red lingerie, glassware, or a sun catcher, for instance.	July Ruby	Think Dorothy in *The Wizard of Oz* and look for ruby-red slippers, jazzy sneakers, or even sparkly flip-flops.
February Amethyst	Present something that's cozy and amethyst-colored, like a lavender pashmina shawl for cuddling up in when it's cold.	August Onyx	Go black and sleek like onyx with a remote-control car or an MP3 player—or a little black dress or a patent-leather purse.
March Aquamarine	Let the ocean inspire your gift: dinner at a seafood restaurant, seashell-decorated jewelry, or a framed seascape, for example.	September Sapphire	Assemble a cocktail kit of martini glasses and gin in a sapphire-blue bottle (left). Finish with an olive-shaped tag.
April Diamond	Play off another meaning of "diamond": give tickets for a baseball game tied to a bag of peanuts in the shell.	October Opal	Have some opalescent fun with a bubble-blowing kit or a bubble-bath set complete with a back-scrubbing brush.
May Emerald	Celebrate the Emerald Isle with a gift of Irish beer—or a trip to the pub—and CDs or downloads of Irish music.	November Topaz	Reflect the golden color of this gem with a selection of favorite white wines, like Chardonnay, Sauvignon Blanc, and Viognier.
June Pearl	Look for pearl-embellished clothes and accessories, like a sweater with pearl buttons or a pearl-beaded evening bag.	December Turquoise	Connect to turquoise's origins in the Southwest with jars of red-hot salsa, a tortilla press, and a Tex-Mex cookbook.

when it's a big one

A milestone birthday is a momentous occasion, so package your present to show that you know the day's a big deal. Fasten a mock set of car keys to a gift for a newly minted driver, or give a friend who's fifty a present with fifty parts.

strength in numbers
Invite family and friends to write down the things they treasure about someone who's turning fifty—for instance, "The way you tell a joke" (above). Gather fifty of those statements of admiration, along with a keepsake card, in a clear container (right). You can also nestle a surprise gift among the slips of paper.

car talk
A car-themed gift zips with red swirl-dot paper and black ribbon that evokes the open road with dashed white lines of correction fluid (left). Double-sided tape keeps a toy car from driving off, and a real key chain secures the gift tag "keys." A car air freshener or fuzzy dice would also make whimsical attachments.

HAPPY BIRTHDAY

50
THINGS
WE ♥
ABOUT YOU

congratulations

When good things happen to people you care about,

congratulations are in order. Recognize a job well done or share

excitement over a new home (or even a new pet) with a thoughtfully

presented gift. It can be as simple as adding a color-coordinated bow

to a cold six-pack or embellishing a box with sparkling stars.

for a job well done

Good news deserves great rewards. Mark an accomplishment by giving a gift that says "I'm proud of you." Star-studded winner's ribbons, cheerleader's pom-poms, and the makings of a Champagne toast are fun ways to celebrate achievement.

way to go!
To cheer someone on, attach red yarn pom-poms to a package wrapped in gold paper (above). Adorn with a red paper star and wispy red and gold cord to suggest a burst of fireworks.

a superstar effort
Decorate a gift bag with silver stars and strips of paper cut to resemble winner's ribbons (left). Add a message, like "You did it!" Consider using stars on gifts in other ways—for instance, adding a row of gold stars. (Remember the stickers your kindergarten teacher used to use?)

make a toast
To acknowledge a success, place a Champagne glass in a tennis-ball tube (far left). Add tinsel and star-shaped confetti to give the illusion of sparklers. Present with a mini bottle of bubbly.

send off a retiree in style

Retirement is a time for diving into favorite hobbies or lifelong dreams of leisure. When someone you love leaves the working world behind, help that person bid adieu with a gift that conjures up all the adventures yet to come.

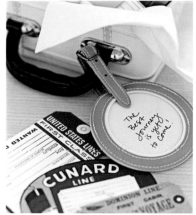

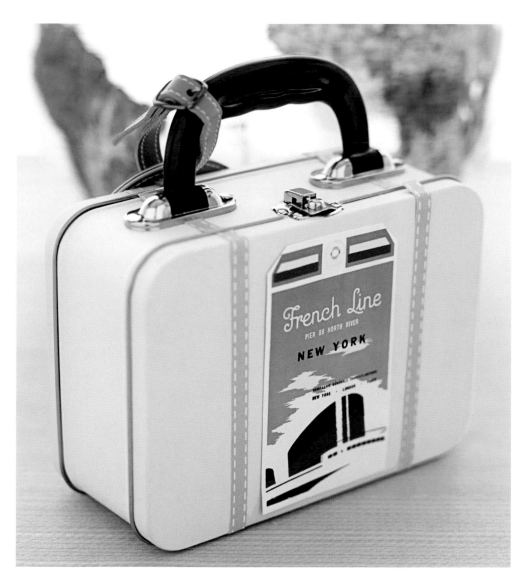

the stuff of dreams

Create a retirement present based on the activities your friend or relative is looking forward to in the next stage of life. For instance, stuff a scaled-down "suitcase" with necessities for a world traveler who's about to take off.

• Decorate a metal lunch box to look like a suitcase from days gone by with a retro-style luggage label and stickers that resemble stitching. (Look at scrapbook supplies for more decorating options.)

• Stow away globe-trotting goodies, like luggage locks, a journal, and an eye mask for sleeping on planes. Customize the stash based on the lucky traveler's itinerary, adding currency, a foreign language dictionary, or plug adapters.

• A luggage tag is a perfect place to wish someone bon voyage, and it can be used later for its original purpose.

raise a mug

Offer caffeinated congratulations to

someone who has been promoted or

made a desired career shift. Fill a mug

with coffee beans and tie on a rock-candy

stir stick to get the first day of a new

job off to a zippy start. Or substitute

tasty treats to brighten the workweek,

such as nuts, pretzels, or candies.

mark a move

Useful gifts, such as home-improvement supplies or frosty cold drinks, are terrific ways to congratulate someone on a move. It's easy to make a housewarming gift special: just tie on a ribbon or use an unusual container, like a paint can.

housewarming gifts

To help celebrate a new home, consider giving a ribbon-tied basket with:

• Mugs, ground coffee, and a French press for that first morning—or until the right kitchen box gets unpacked.

• A copy of *It's a Wonderful Life* and the film's symbols of home and hearth: bread, wine, and salt (so that life will always have flavor).

bring refreshment
Help christen a new home by arriving with an ice-cold six-pack of root beer (left) or another favorite beverage. To make the presentation special, cover the carton with kraft paper and add a ribbon that complements the bottle caps.

canned goods
Fill a paint can with essentials for a new home (far left), like sprucing-up supplies or handy household items, such as tape, batteries, and lightbulbs. (Hardware and home-improvement stores sell paint cans.) To decorate, tape paint swatches around the can and tie with twine.

for a furry new friend

Congratulate a pal on a new four-legged addition to the family by wrapping practical gifts for the pet in a way that's fun for the owner. Add whimsical touches like paw prints.

fancy footprints

Serve up cat toys in a food dish (left). Tie on a matching ribbon embellished with dots in patterns to look like paw prints. (These circles are made of adhesive felt and sold for protecting floors.) Cats also love to chase light beams, so consider tucking in a laser pointer or a flashlight for interactive play.

bone up

Present a trio of rawhide bones in bright striped tissue paper (right), with a collar to hold it all together. A dog tag that says "good dog" makes a clever gift tag. You can also buy a kit to make a tag or order one with a personalized message at a pet store. Snip the ends of the tissue paper to create fringe.

welcome, neighbors

Make the folks who just moved in feel right at home with a gift of insider information: menus from your favorite local restaurants. Package the menus like a take-out meal, and your gift might open the door for future dinners together.

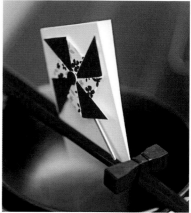

show them the ropes

There are few presents more personal than sharing your neighborhood secrets with the new kids on the block.

● Fill a Chinese food container with fortune cookies, chopsticks, and, most important, menus from tried-and-true local restaurants, from the best Chinese take-out place to the corner diner.

● To embellish the gift, add Asian-style bowls and slip an origami-inspired gift tag between two chopsticks.

● You can also collect take-out menus with your favorite dishes highlighted in a folder, a binder, or a large envelope.

grand occasions

Life's major milestones—a marriage, the birth of a child,

a wedding anniversary—call for distinctive gifts dressed up in

remarkable ways. Going all out with the presentation of your gifts

shows how happy you are for the people you're honoring,

so go ahead and wrap your packages with panache.

showering the bride

It's fun to buy (and watch a bride-to-be open) multiple wedding shower gifts, whether gadgets for the kitchen or lingerie for her trousseau. Wrap each item individually and bundle them all together in a larger decorated box.

group effort

A gift box filled with lots of smaller packages prolongs the excitement of unwrapping. Decorate both the large and small boxes in the same color palette, such as pink with white accents.

● For the box, consider a nontraditional shape, such as an octagon. Cover the sides with embossed paper, leaving the top open to showcase the gifts inside.

● Trim pink tissue paper with pinking shears and line the box with it, arranging the tissue to peek out the top.

● Wrap the packages and trim with buttons, paper-flower appliqués, and ribbons of varying textures, like pink pom-poms on metallic string.

● As a sweet embellishment, enclose a nosegay of tiny fresh flowers.

gifts for the bridal party

Show the members of your bridal party how much you appreciate them with presents that recognize their important roles in your big day.

surrounded by friends

Give the people standing up for you the attention they deserve by encircling packages with a band of guys or gals (left). Cut dolls from paper and glue on paper clothes, such as these mod black-and-white dresses and black tuxedos. You can tailor the dolls' outfits to match what your attendants will actually be wearing on your wedding day.

wax sentimental

Gold sealing wax, showing the bride's new initials, fastens crossed metallic ribbons and offers a contemporary take on monograms (right). This elegant look, which is perfect for bridesmaids' gifts, would also suit smaller thank-you gifts—for the musicians, the florist, or the photographer, for example.

wedding wishes

A marriage celebration warrants taking the time to create memorable packaging for a gift. By wrapping boxes in shimmering colors or tiering them like a wedding cake, you show the bride and groom how much you care.

shades of elegance
As an alternative to white, choose a palette of blue, bronze, and gold (left and above) for a wedding gift. Create a striped effect with three bands of layered ribbons. Finish with a generously looped bow, a sprig of fresh flowers, and a tag attached with a string of glass beads.

it takes the cake
Stack a trio of presents in circular boxes to resemble a wedding cake (right). Secure the tiers with glue or double-sided tape and cover the seams with beaded-flower ribbon or other bridal notions. Top it off with wide, sheer ribbon tied in a loose, cascading bow.

Best Wishes

crafting paper flowers

Blossoms abound everywhere at weddings—the ceremony site, the bouquets, the reception tables. Decorate your wedding gift with flowers, too—the kind made from delicate tissue. Here's how to make a present bloom with a bouquet of fond wishes.

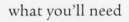

what you'll need

Reflect the colors of real flowers in your tissue ones.

- Square box
- Wrapping paper
- Wired fabric ribbon
- Tissue paper in three shades, such as yellow, gold, and white
- Thin wire, such as jewelry or florist's wire

budding flower design

Wrap the box in paper, tie a multilooped bow using wired ribbon, and top with tissue-paper flowers.

1 Fold sheets of tissue paper and, starting at the folds, cut petal shapes in at least three sizes from small (center of flower) to large (outside petals).

2 Pinch a small petal shape at the fold. Holding it in your fingers, pinch and add more petals from small to large—until the flower is the size you want.

3 Secure the bottom of the flower by winding thin wire around the base. Using your fingers, fluff the petals into the desired flower shape.

4 Repeat the previous steps to craft at least four flowers—more if you'd like—then tape your handmade blooms around the bow. (Using wired ribbon to tie the bow makes it easier for the loops to pop out above the paper flowers.)

anniversary gift themes

Remember a wedding anniversary, whether yours or another couple's,
with a gift that's inspired by a traditional or contemporary theme.

year	traditional	contemporary	year	traditional	contemporary
1	Paper Framed lyrics of "your song"	Clocks A dual alarm or time-zone clock	15	Crystal A crystal carafe and red wine	Watches A fitness or GPS watch
2	Cotton A monogrammed, thick terry bathrobe	China The serving piece that's still missing	20	China A pair of teacups with a tea press	Platinum A platinum album by a favorite artist
3	Leather A leather-bound book or keepsake box	Glass, crystal A glass or crystal ornament	25	Silver An engraved silver ice bucket and Champagne	Silver Matching silver key rings
4	Fruit, flowers An Apple iPod loaded with favorite songs	Appliances A two-serving cappuccino maker	30	Pearl Pearl-handled knives or serving utensils	Diamond Sometimes only the real thing will do
5	Wood A tree or vine in a wooden planter (right)	Silverware A set of deluxe grilling tools	40	Ruby A set of cordial glasses and ruby port	Garnet A cashmere throw in garnet red
10	Tin Tin lanterns with candles	Diamond Jewelry in a diamond shape—or the real thing	50	Gold A gold picture frame and a photography session	Gold A scrapbook with gold leaf–bordered pages

1980
First date

1982
Got hitched

1984
It's a boy!

1985
First (tiny!) house

1987
It's a girl!

1988
Bigger house

1997
Camping in Europe

2002
Ben goes to college

2005
Lisa goes to college

2006
Alaskan cruise

2007
25 YEARS!

celebrate a couple

When wrapping a gift for a special couple's anniversary, add decorations that reflect memories of their life together. Embellishments like a framed wedding photo or a time line of the couple's relationship spotlight their happy union.

picture perfect

Remind a couple of their rich history together with a framed wedding photo hung on the outside of an anniversary gift (left). Wrap the box like a wedding present in cream-and-white checkered paper and textured ribbons in silver and cream satin (above).

anniversary toast

Make a boxed bottle of bubbly (far left) even more celebratory with a time line of milestones in the couple's relationship. Print a list of the events. Trim the paper and hole-punch the edges to look like bubbles rising in a Champagne glass. Attach the time line to the box with double-sided tape.

getting ready for baby

Part of the fun of a baby shower is watching a mom-to-be open her presents. Your gift is sure to make the guests ooh and aah when you add on adorable accessories, such as a yellow rubber ducky or sweetly patterned teddy-bear tags.

more shower gifts

Give baby necessities in a container that's also a gift:

• A small caddy with a handle, with diapers, wipes, and ointment.

• A white wicker laundry basket, with baby-friendly detergent, unscented dryer sheets, and mini hangers.

• A cloth baby carrier, with a sun hat, sunglasses, and other outdoor gear.

just ducky
A rubber duck swims in a bubble bath of white ribbon—just nestle the toy in a premade bow (left). When you don't know yet if it's a boy or a girl, a colorful geometric pattern (like this checkerboard print) and white rickrack are fun options.

a mother's touch
Blankets for both the mom-to-be and her child give a nod to the softer side of motherhood (right). Fold a lap throw and a baby blankie, tie each with a fabric ribbon, and tuck in tags for Mama Bear and Baby Bear. You can also present hand-knit clothing in a similar fashion.

go blue—or think pink

Welcome a baby boy or girl with a present decked out in darling attachments that can be used later to decorate the nursery or to keep little toes toasty warm.

over the moon

Tailor a gingham-wrapped present for little boy blue (right) with a miniature shirt that shows off his new name in painted wooden letters. (Craft stores sell similar letters and shapes.) A ribbon makes it easy to hang the personalized decoration on a nursery wall.

shake your booties

Mini clothespins attach baby socks to a string clothesline on a pink box (far right), which holds a gift for a baby girl now—and can hold mementos later. Thread wide ribbon through a diaper pin with alphabet beads spelling out her name. Top with booties in a mesh bag.

appreciation

Sometimes you want a present to say a straightforward and

heartfelt "thank you." Other times, you want it to convey a specific

message of appreciation like "Thanks for inviting me into your home"

or simply "I was thinking of you." Whatever the situation, the way you

present a gift shows how much you appreciate the recipient.

just because

There doesn't have to be a specific occasion to give a gift to someone who's special to you, and a "just because" gift can be small. But when you present it, use novel attachments like glass beads and wooden buttons to make it extra enticing.

accents from nature

Natural decorations please the eye and tease our senses of smell and touch.

• Garnish a gift with lavender or herb sprigs.

• Write an inspirational word on a smooth stone. Wrap wire around the stone, then around a gift.

• Glue or wire pieces of sea glass to a package.

beaded beauties
Colorful glass beads decorate soap rounds covered in textured paper (left). String the beads onto thin florist's or jewelry wire and wind it around and around the package like ribbon.

cleverly crafted
Brown kraft paper is anything but plain when adorned with thin stitched ribbon threaded through wooden buttons (right). The circle gift tag echoes the shape of the buttons. This simple but sweet treatment is great for dressing up small gifts like note cards or candles.

turn notes into presents

It doesn't take much to transform cards into gifts. Fond sentiments, presented in decorated envelopes, show your friends just how much they're treasured.

flowery language

Wrap ribbons around thank-you notes (left) to transform them into gifts. To make "roses," roll strips of tissue paper, pinch one end, then fluff the other to create a bud. Secure and attach to the card with wired ribbon.

give them butterflies

Thin brown ribbon tied on an angle (right) turns thank-you notes into treats. To play up the note cards' garden motif, attach fluttery butterflies. (These appliqués are scrapbook supplies; stickers or paper cutouts will also work.) Brown, baby blue, and chartreuse offer a contemporary color combination.

giving bags of thanks

An elegant bag, elegantly presented, is

a fitting way to show your appreciation

to a woman who's done something

special for you. Slip a pretty present like

a beaded purse inside a sheer bag, so its

sparkles and pattern peek through, then

tie it closed with satin ribbon. Include a

stylish note trimmed with a fabric flower.

good wine for great friends

When you arrive for dinner with a fine bottle of wine, your host or hostess has yet another reason to raise a glass to you. Wrap the bottle so it's fit for a connoisseur.

tasteful cover-ups

Napkins can be nifty as wrappers for wine bottles (right). Bundle a cloth napkin around the bottom of a bottle and tie with a sheer ribbon. Add an extra, like a bottle stopper. Or cover the top of a bottle with a paper cocktail napkin, and finish with ribbon and a gift tag cut into a wine-bottle shape.

ribbon wrap

Weave a ribbon "bag" (far right) by crossing four wide ribbons under a bottle and pulling up both sides of each one; tape at the top. Leave both ends of one ribbon long and trim the rest. Weave shorter ribbons in horizontal rows through the vertical ribbons. Finish by tying the long strands into a bow.

hostess gifts to savor

When invited to dinner or a party, it's thoughtful to bring a present for the host or hostess. A bottle of wine or flowers are always nice, but so are sweet or savory treats. Choose something delicious, then package it in an unexpected way.

citrus surprise

A bowl of lemons tied with a burlap bow (above) is a refreshing contribution to a summer party. As an extra, line the bowl with a colorful dish towel or tie on a citrus press. Adapt this gift to the season by bringing apples to a fall get-together or clementines to a holiday brunch.

delicious dipping

Trim a bottle of olive oil with ribbon and olive-leaf gift tags cut from paper (left). Consider presenting the oil with a bottle of balsamic vinegar or a dipping bowl filled with fresh herbs, such as rosemary. For a cookout, package a similar gift of barbecue sauce and a basting brush.

indulge her

A gift of shortbread cookies nestled in a keepsake teacup (far left) lets the hostess relax and enjoy a cup of tea with a treat after the party. Include a tea bag in a soothing blend like chamomile or tie on a teaspoon for a practical decoration.

holidays

Holidays sprinkle joy around the calendar—and offer

lots of opportunities to share that joy with the people you care about.

Whether you're giving presents for Valentine's Day, Easter, Hanukkah,

or Christmas, adorn your offerings with personal and seasonal touches

to make giving and receiving them all the more memorable.

be my valentine

When giving chocolate—the quintessential Valentine's Day gift—offer a twist on an old favorite and give the bar a more personal wrapper. Passion doesn't thrive on chocolate alone: this present is even sweeter when you wrap it in a love letter.

share your sentiments

Valentine's Day is the ideal time to show your love by giving a sweet treat enveloped in even sweeter sentiments.

● Remove the paper wrapper from a chocolate bar (or several, if you'd like to multiply your sentiments). Wrap a piece of writing paper and a piece of gift wrap around the bar (or bars) and cut to size.

● Write a love note on the writing paper and place it face up on the inside of the gift wrap. With the gift wrap on the outside, wrap both pieces of paper around the chocolate. Seal with a sticker.

● Encircle the bar with velvet ribbon. Use a coil of wire and a cutout heart to make a three-dimensional gift tag.

● You can slip other goodies, like tickets to a concert or sporting event, into the layers of wrapping—or tuck in a brochure from that quaint bed-and-breakfast where you'll be taking your sweetie.

valentines for all ages

Delight a young cherub with a plush friend peeking out of a custom-cut gift bag. Treat older cupids to simply and sweetly wrapped candies.

tiny treats

Cradle chocolates in miniature baking cups, cover in tulle, and tie with thin satin ribbon (left). Presenting a tray of individually wrapped candies is an easy way to offer treats to an entire classroom or office. These cups are silicone, but you can also look in a supermarket baking section for paper or foil options.

peekaboo plush

A teddy bear peers out of a gift bag's heart-shaped window (right). To create this effect, cut a shape in the side of a gift bag. Candy-colored tissue paper provides soft surroundings. Attach a heart-shaped valentine for a present that's sure to earn a big bear hug.

rethinking easter baskets

Easter arrives with spring, the season of rebirth. Take a new approach to Easter baskets by planting the bunny's bounty in unexpected containers, like clear or round boxes, and filling with fresh flowers—or candies shaped like flowers.

other basket ideas

Think beyond the basket to hatch creative Easter gifts.

• Nestle gifts in sand pails amid shredded paper.

• Line oversized mugs with tissue and add treats.

• Decorate an egg carton with paint or stickers and fill it with small candies.

• Stuff a pastel cloth sack with Easter surprises.

boxed treats
Fill a clear plastic box with shredded paper and border it with fringed paper "grass" (left). Buy cellophane-covered candies clustered in the shape of flowers (shown here) or make your own by taping or wiring the wrappers of candies together (cover wire with florist's tape). Sprinkle in floral-colored candies such as Jordan almonds or jelly beans.

hop into spring
Cover a round kraft box (right) with bunny-and-flower-print paper and trim with pink cording. Line with tissue, then fill with candy eggs, or stone ones like these. Finish with a just-picked flower.

celebrating hanukkah

To make the Festival of Lights even brighter, use metallic accents. String shiny-numbered packages together with sparkling cord or give traditional candy coins in silver foil.

one for each night

Eight gifts in blue boxes tantalizingly tagged with silver numbers (left) provide eight days' worth of wonder. Connected by a silver cord, the boxes can sit near a menorah as a decorative reminder of Hanukkah's traditions.

silver standard

Popular Hanukkah treats are chocolate gelt, foil-covered candy coins. Tuck gelt wrapped in silver foil into iridescent blue bags and tie with a blue ribbon to display traditional Hanukkah colors in a modern way (right).

make it personal

Christmas is a great time to introduce a signature wrapping style, which you can then use year-round. Your distinctively wrapped presents will stand out under the tree, and people will know immediately which of their gifts are from you.

express yourself

When everyone knows which packages are from you before looking at the tags, you've got a signature wrapping style. If you don't have one already, try using metallic wrap and bows with three loops.

● Wrap gifts in silver or gold paper and adorn with looped circles of wired ribbon, which is easy to shape. The wire also helps the loops hold their form from the time you wrap the presents until they're opened. Use double-sided tape to keep the loops in place, then attach to the package with ribbon.

● Crisscross ribbons and thin metallic strands in unexpected spots or weave several around a package. Add circular gift tags to round out the theme.

● Define a trademark style by relying on the same gift wrap, whether solid or patterned; picking a single color or just a few colors; or choosing an icon or ribbon style to feature on every gift you give.

wrapped up
all cozy

Reflect the warmth of the Christmas season with gift wrap that has the look or feel of cozy fabric. Add classic holiday hardware such as jingle bells and wooden ornaments.

bundle up
Lend boxes the appeal of a favorite sweater by using a color copier to make gift wrap (left). Copy a warm, woolly sweater in red and white stripes or a green cable knit, for example. Wrap with the resulting paper, and add sparkle with strands of jingle bells.

let it snow
Stuff a tree-decked felt bag with shredded paper and plenty of presents (right). Tied on with fabric ribbon featuring a holiday message, a wooden snowflake serves as an accent, a tag, and a tree ornament.

festive cookie containers

Make friends and neighbors think—and taste—Christmas with baked-at-home cookies. Glue a snowflake cut from gold paper on the tin, and capture the twinkle of fresh snow with shiny metallic yarn crisscrossed to look like another festive flake. Or use different holiday icons, like stars or snowmen, for your cookie tin.

they'll never guess!

Some people see wrapped gifts and just have to investigate. Foil their squeezing and shaking with wily wrapping that disguises a package's true contents. Place small gifts inside larger containers, and throw in bells to throw them off track.

what you'll need

Opt for gift wrap that doesn't hint at the gift—no musical notes for an iPod!

- Small box and larger box

- Gift wrap

- Ribbon

- Shredded paper

- Jingle bells

- Pepper berries

keep it under wraps

Outwit squeezers, shakers, and snoopers, and enhance their excitement over your present, by camouflaging this year's easy-to-guess gift.

1 Wrap the real gift in its own box. Place the wrapped gift inside a larger box, thus keeping someone from knowing its true size and shape and whether it's soft or hard. Because this real gift is square, a round box adds to the mystery.

2 Fill the larger box with shredded paper or other padding. Then add plenty of jingle bells. All the shakers will hear are the sounds of Santa's sled.

3 Wrap the larger box. For a round box, wrap a strip of gift wrap around the side of the box, then cover the lid with different paper and edge with ribbon. (For another way to wrap a round box, see page 137.) To finish, add pepper berries to a bow.

merry attachments

Add an extra layer of cheer to a Christmas present with a holiday-inspired accent that reflects the shapes, colors, and joys of the season. Bake a gingerbread man, gather a sprig of holly berries, or hand-stitch a satin-trimmed gift tag.

happy holly
A sprig of holly berries and leaves tied with a red ribbon lends Christmas spirit to a box wrapped in candy cane–striped paper (above). You can also attach an ornament, jingle bells, pinecones, or small branches of yuletide greenery.

sweet fella
Fasten a jolly gingerbread man to a gift. Red-and-white striped ribbon picks up the color of the red candy buttons (left). To make it easier to attach cookies to a package, poke holes in the dough before baking. (Be sure to make the holes large enough so that they don't close up when you bake the cookies.)

shapes of the season
Tag a gift warmly with a stocking cut out of heavy paper (right). Stitch striped gift wrap onto the heel and the toe with embroidery floss, and add sheen with a cuff of satin ribbon. To simplify making gift tags in shapes such as trees, stars, and bells, trace cookie cutters.

presenting gift cards

Create excitement over gift cards by packaging them in surprising ways. Hint at the shopping fun to come by placing the cards in miniature shopping bags on the tree, or dress up gift-card boxes with sparkling garlands.

glittering garlands
Metallic trims—textured ribbon, sequined wire flowers, tinsel strands, and beaded string (above)—add sparkling holiday cheer to pillow boxes that hold gift cards (right). A wrapped gift card also makes a nice tag on a larger, related present.

in the bag
Surprise them on Christmas morning with gift cards from Santa on the tree. Cover the cards with gift wrap and stow in clear mini bags (left). Slip in strips of silver paper to show who the gift cards are for, then hang from the tree's branches or set in its boughs.

how-to

All it takes to wrap a gift that makes someone say "wow" is a

little know-how—and some gift-wrapping essentials. If you keep your

supply of boxes, bows, and wrap well stocked, update it frequently, and

have a few wrapping tips at hand, you'll be ready to put together

a memorable gift presentation any time the occasion arises.

get ready to wrap

Whether your gift-wrap stash fills a box or a closet, keeping both the basics and some special extras on hand makes it easy to create custom presentations.

containers	wrapping paper	ribbons & bows
Boxes, bags, and other containers provide the foundation when you're wrapping gifts. Stow away a supply of the following:	Paper in solid colors and simple patterns works well for many occasions. If you fall in love with a paper, stock up and make it your signature. Some must-haves:	A package gets its personality from ribbons and bows. Give yourself the flexibility to be inventive with a selection of colors, widths, and textures:
• Plain and occasion-specific gift bags • Shirt and sweater boxes • Jewelry-size boxes • Kraft and other premade boxes, such as round hatboxes	• Solid and striped gift wrap • Holiday and birthday gift wrap • Kraft and construction paper • Tissue paper in several colors	• Premade bows • Curling ribbon • A variety of fabric ribbons, including wired ones • Cording, yarn, and twine

gift tags	attachments	art supplies & tools
Beyond traditional gift tags, stash away options like metal-rimmed paper key tags, luggage tags, and greeting cards that you can trim with pinking shears. Also include:	Items that embellish a package can become part of the present. Put aside pretty little things for attaching to gifts:	To supplement the basics, reach for tools and materials that will encourage your creativity:
• Tags that match your gift wrap • Occasion-specific tags • Enclosure cards • Heavy paper, such as card stock, for making custom tags	• Cookie cutters and ornaments • Beads, buttons, and brooches • Metal and wooden shapes, numbers, and letters • Small kitchen gadgets, like wine stoppers or mini whisks	• Rubber stamps and ink pads • An assortment of stickers • Metallic and colored pens • Hole punch and pinking shears • Glue and double-sided tape • Florist's or jewelry wire

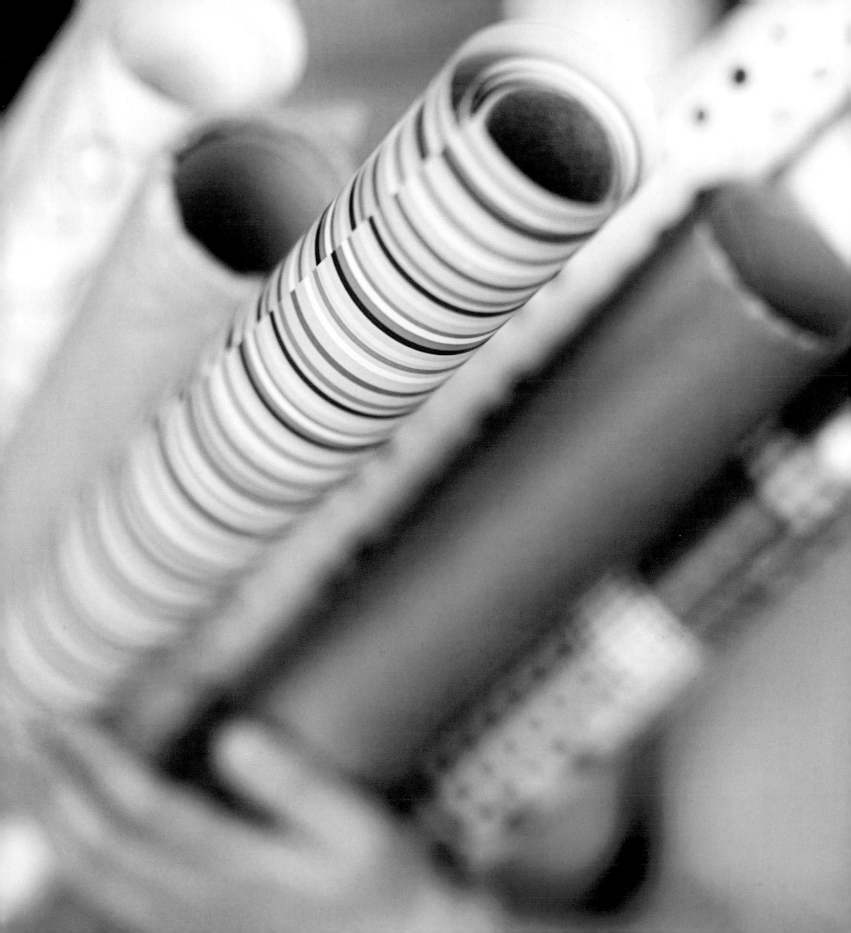

wrapping boxes

Create a perfect fit between gift wrap and a square or rectangular box with a few crisp folds and double-sided tape (the professionals' secret weapon).

square box

To measure and position wrapping paper for a square box, place the box upside down on the paper. Wrap the paper around the box so that the edges overlap by at least 1 inch on each side and cut. Trim the paper on the ends so that it is about two-thirds of the box's height.

1 Secure the paper around the box with double-sided tape at the seam. Fold down one end; trim remaining paper so the sides will meet in the middle in step 2.

2 Making crisp creases, fold in one trimmed side of the paper and secure with tape; repeat with the other side. The remaining paper forms a triangular flap.

3 Place double-sided tape on the inside of the triangular flap and press it snugly against the box. Repeat the steps on the opposite end of the box.

---

rectangular box

To measure and position gift wrap for a rectangular box, place the box upside down on the paper. Wrap the paper around the box so that the edges overlap by 1 inch on each side and cut. (For a neater finish, leave 2 inches on each side and fold the cut edges under.) The paper on the ends should be about two-thirds of the box's height.

1 Secure the paper around the box with double-sided tape at the seam. Push in the sides of the paper that stick out on one end.

2 Place double-sided tape on the inside of the flap on top (this will be the bottom flap when you're done) and press it against the box. Because the cut edge of the other flap will show when the box is completely wrapped, fold it over slightly for a neat finish.

3 Place double-sided tape on the inside of the folded flap and press it snugly against the box. Repeat the steps on the opposite end of the box.

wrapping odd-shaped gifts

Don't let an unusual container or object throw your wrapping off course. Here's how to fit paper beautifully around a gift that doesn't come in an everyday box.

cylinder or round box

Pretty pleating makes it a snap to wrap cylinders or round boxes. Start by measuring: place the container on its side, roll in gift wrap to cover, and cut, leaving a 1-inch overlap. (For another method of wrapping a round box, see page 125.)

1 The edges of the paper that hang over should cover a little more than half of the container's ends; trim, if necessary. Fasten the seam with double-sided tape.

2 Pleat edges of paper in small sections to lie flat, moving around the circle until all pieces are folded down in a fan-like shape. Repeat on the other end.

3 Secure the paper at each end with a sticker large enough to cover the edges of the fan folds (see photo, page 130). Or tape the paper and put a bow on top.

odd shape

Gifts that come in unconventional shapes, like plush toys, can be wrapped without too much fuss. The secrets are to use soft paper or fabric and to place the gift on a solid base to serve as the foundation for your wrapping.

1 Cut a circle out of cardboard, making sure that the circle is slightly bigger than the bottom of the object you're wrapping.

2 Place the circle in the center of a sheet of gift wrap, several layers of tissue paper, or a piece of soft fabric, then put the gift item on the circle.

3 Pull up the sides of the paper or fabric, shorter sides first, then longer sides to cover. Cinch partway down and tie with ribbon.

tying bows

Sure, tying a bow can be as simple as tying your shoes. But making an especially neat and pretty bow—or tying one with lots of loops—needn't be a challenge, either.

basic bow

There's a trick to tying a ribbon so you end up with a cleanly finished bow. This technique brings a piece of ribbon in front of the knot, rather than taking the ribbon behind it as most of us do when tying shoelaces.

1 Crisscross the ribbon around the box, crossing underneath and knotting on top. Pinch a loop in the loose ribbon end that comes out on the bottom of the knot.

2 Bring the other end of the ribbon down to cover where you've pinched the loop, push it underneath that loop, and pull through to create the second loop.

3 Pull loops tight to finish the bow. Trim ends to make sure they are even and neat. (For ends as pictured, fold ribbon width in half, then cut at an angle.)

multiloop bow

This method transforms ribbon into a blossoming bow that will give extra oomph to your package. All it takes is a lot of loops and two pieces of ribbon (preferably wired, to best hold its shape).

1 Fold a long piece of ribbon back and forth into S shapes to create a stack of four to six loops that resembles ribbon candy.

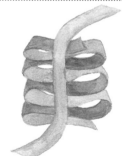

2 Tie a second, short piece of ribbon tight around the middle of the stack of loops and knot. Hide the knot below the stack.

3 Fluff out the loops and attach the bow to the gift. (If you've crisscrossed ribbon around a box, use the ends to tie on the bow.)

INDEX

thanks

acknowledgments

All photography by Aimée Herring except for the following:

Hallmark Cards, Inc., pages 117 and 126.

Weldon Owen wishes to thank everyone at Hallmark who contributed ideas, support, and enthusiasm for this book, especially Peg Anderson-Lee, Court Babcock, Lisa Beel, Stacey Bishop, Patty Cheong, Sirpa Cowell, Bet David, Mary Emanuel, Gretchen Finch, Mary Gentry, Cheryl Graham, Todd Hafer, Chelsea Hunziker, Joyce Jennings, Ruth Kanai, Jeff Morgan, Monica Obando, Tracey Petrie, Linda Posey, Sara Powell-Moody, Jane-Elyse Pryor, Brad Rinehart, Dee Roof, Stacy Schaffer, Becky Smith, Kevin Swanson, Lisa Tobin, Theresa Trinder, Karen Turner, and Megan Walsh.

We gratefully acknowledge design assistance from Anna Migirova, Britt Staebler, and Kelly Booth. Special thanks to Renée Myers for supporting the styling team. We would also like to thank the following people for contributing to the production of this book:

Copy Editor: Jacqueline K. Aaron. Proofreaders: Peter Cieply, Marisa Solís, Sharron Wood. Indexer: Ken DellaPenta. Photography Assistant: Laura Flippen. Stylist's Assistant: Daniele Maxwell. Homeowners: The Brian Griggs Family, David Johnson, and Brad and Marsha Quanstrom. Models: Dale and Garret Conour; Julia Nelson; Charlie and Tommy Quanstrom.

If you have enjoyed this book,
Hallmark would love to hear from you.

Please send comments to:
Book Feedback
2501 McGee, Mail Drop 215
Kansas City, MO 64141-6580

or e-mail us at:
booknotes@hallmark.com

www.hallmark.com

May all the gifts you give
bring special happiness to
you and those you love.